FOR THE LOVE OF *The* CUBS

Written by Frederick C. Klein

Illustration and Design by Mark Anderson

Foreword by Pat Hughes

This book combines two of the things that are most important in my life–helping children learn and baseball. When I was a kid growing up, I learned my math and improved my spelling by collecting baseball cards, and I think that *For the Love of the Cubs* can help children in a similar way. What better way to help a child learn the ABCs than by simultaneously learning the history, players, and coaches of the Chicago Cubs? It is so much fun and it is such an honor to watch and talk about the Chicago Cubs during the season, but I realize that there is a lot to know about the Cubs. Learning to spell and learning history is all about words on a page, which can be hard to remember. But in *For the Love of the Cubs*, the illustrations bring those words and the team's history to life right before your eyes. I hope that you and your children enjoy *For the Love of the Cubs* as much as my wife and I have enjoyed sharing the book with our two daughters.

–**Pat Hughes**,
WSCR AM Radio play-by-play voice of the Cubs

"That ball's got a chaaaance!"

"A" is for the Architects

Theo and Ricketts,
They've got Cubs' fans purchasing
Postseason tickets

Tom Ricketts, a native of Omaha, Nebraska, and a graduate of the University of Chicago, purchased the Cubs in 2009 from the Tribune Company, pledging to help the team achieve the playing-field success that had eluded it for almost a century. In 2012, Ricketts hired as his head of baseball operations **Theo Epstein**, who had already guided the Boston Red Sox to World Series victories in 2004 and 2007, ending their 86-year championship drought. Epstein rebuilt the Cubs from the ground up, molding a young, dynamic roster that promises to add more World Series trophies to the team's breakthrough, 2016 triumph.

"B" is for Ernie Banks,

The "Let's Play Two" man.
At shortstop or first,
Number one with the fans.

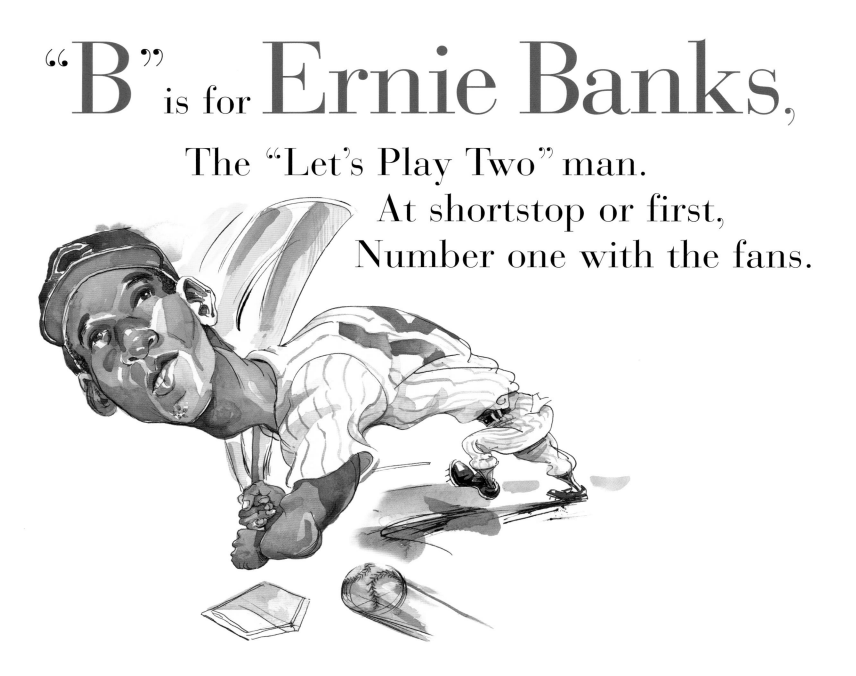

Ernie Banks played with the Cubs as a shortstop or first baseman from 1953 through 1971. He was the club's career home-run leader, with 512, for over 40 years. His cheerful disposition and love for the game made him a fan favorite. He's a member of the Baseball Hall of Fame, and a pennant bearing his uniform number, 14, flies from a flagpole at Wrigley Field.

"C" is for Harry Caray

His accounts never dragged.
He made the games Fun
Even when the Cubs lagged.

Harry Caray was the Cubs' main television voice from 1982 through 1997. He was a fun-loving man whose colorful language and enthusiasm for baseball made his broadcasts distinctive. A statue of him, leading the crowd in singing "Take Me Out to the Ballgame," stands outside Wrigley Field.

"D" is for Double Play–

Baez and Russell,
A combo that generates
a whole lotta hustle.

From Tinker and Evers to Dunston and Sandberg, the Cubs have had many notable shortstop–second base double-play combinations over the decades; the Russell-Baez pair ranks with them for effectiveness, if not longevity. Shortstop **Addison Russell**, the 11th player picked in the 2012 draft, has quickly established himself as one of the game's premier players at his demanding position, flashing exceptional range and batting power. His grand-slam sparked the Cubs' victory over the Cleveland Indians in Game 6 of the 2016 World Series. Second-baseman **Javier Baez** was the Cubs top choice in the 2011 draft. A jack-of-all-trades in the field, and with a knack for the spectacular both there and at the plate, he became a one-man highlights reel during the Cubs' playoffs run.

"E" is for Johnny Evers,

Who with Tinker and Chance, made a trio that could turn a double play in a glance.

Second baseman Johnny Evers, shortstop Joe Tinker, and first baseman Frank Chance were the best players on the Cubs teams that won National League pennants in 1906, 1907, 1908, and 1910, and the World Series in 1907 and 1908. All three are in the Hall of Fame. Thanks partly to a poem about them, Tinker-to-Evers-to-Chance remains baseball's most famous double-play combination.

"F" is for First Basemen.

Few teams have had better
Than Charlie Grimm,
Mark Grace, Or Phil Cavarretta.

"Jolly Cholly" Grimm starred at first base for the Cubs from 1925 through 1936 and managed the team to its 1935 and 1945 pennants. MARK GRACE manned the position for 13 seasons ending in 2000; his 1,754 hits during the 1990s led the Major Leagues. Chicago-native PHIL CAVARRETTA was the National League's leading hitter and Most Valuable Player for the 1945 NL champs.

"G" is for Goat

From a long line of billies.
His owner's vile curse,
No more gives fans the willies.

William Sianis, owner of Chicago's Billy Goat tavern, appeared at Wrigley Field for the fourth game of the 1945 World Series, between the Cubs and the Detroit Tigers, accompanied by his pet goat. Sianis displayed two box-seat tickets and asked that he and the goat be seated. They were, but after the game began they were ejected, reportedly at the insistence of Cubs' owner P.K. Wrigley, who said the animal smelled bad. Sianis left but said he hoped the Cubs never played another World Series at the ballpark. In 2016, the curse was obliterated.

"H" is for "Hey! Hey!"

–Jack Brickhouse's yell.
Few mike men did baseball
nearly as well.

Jack Brickhouse was the Cubs' featured broadcaster from 1948 through 1981, a period of 33 years. He was popular with fans because of his cheerful personality and love of the team. He'd cry "Hey! Hey!" when a Cub hit a home run or the team won a game.

"I" is for Innings

The standard is nine.
But if the game's tied,
Then more are just fine.

"J" is for Fergie
Jenkins,

A Canadian lad.
Six 20-win seasons
Showed what he had.

Ferguson Jenkins came to the Cubs in a 1966 trade and won 20 or more games in six of the next eight seasons. The tall right-handed pitcher was traded away in 1974 but returned in 1982 to play his last two seasons in Chicago. Of his 284 career victories, 167 were with the Cubs. In 1991 he became the first Canadian-born player elected to the Hall of Fame.

"K" is for Kyle Hendricks

Who sets batters to chase;
All his keen, off-speed stuff
Has made him an ace.

Nicknamed "The Professor" for his Ivy League collegiate background, Kyle Hendricks was acquired by the Cubs in a 2012 trade with the Texas Rangers for Ryan Dempster, a then-popular Cubs' starter who was out of baseball a year later. Hendricks was picked in the 8th round of the 2011 draft out of Dartmouth College, from which he later would graduate. He led the National League in earned-run-average (2.13) in 2016 and his seven shutout innings in Game 6 of the League Championship Series against the Los Angeles Dodgers helped win the pennant for the Cubs.

"L" is for Left Field,

A position for power.
Billy Williams played there,
And Kingman and Sauer.

Home run-hitting left fielders have been a Cubs' tradition. Billy Williams (pictured at right) started at the position from 1961 through 1974 and hit 392 homers, ranking third on the team's all-time list in that department. Hank Sauer led the National League in home runs in 1952 while playing left field, and Dave Kingman did the same thing in 1979.

"M" is for Mordecai

"Three Finger" Brown.
When the batters came up
He'd sit 'em right down.

Mordecai Brown lost part of the index finger on his right throwing hand in a boyhood farm accident, but contemporaries said that helped make his curveball nastier. He won 20 or more games for the Cubs every year from 1906 through 1911, and a total of five games for the team in the 1906, 1907, 1908, and 1910 World Series, three of them by shutout.

"N" is for Bill Nicholson

They called him "Big Swish."
He struck out as often
As a pitcher could wish.

"O" is for Billy Ott

He played fairly well. But the Cubs wished
they'd had The Ott who was Mel.

Billy Ott was a part-time outfielder for the Cubs in 1962 and 1964, his only seasons in the major leagues. He is in this book to show that most big leaguers have short careers, and aren't stars. Of the more than 1,700 players who've worn a Cubs uniform, many played for one season or less. Mel Ott, on the other hand, was one of the game's leading hitters in a 22-year career with the New York Giants, the Cubs' main rival in the twenties and thirties. **Bill Nicholson played right field for the Cubs from 1939 through 1948.** He got his nickname because he struck out a lot, but he also hit many home runs, leading the league in 1943 and 1944. His eight RBIs led the team during the 1945 World Series, which they lost to the Detroit Tigers in seven games.

"P" is for Power

It's in Kris Bryant's bat.
When he connects, folks marvel:
"Did he really do that?!"

Kris Bryant was only 24 years old when the 2016 season began but already needed an annex to house his awards. The native of Las Vegas, Nevada, was a three-time All-American at third base for the University of San Diego, MVP of the Arizona Fall League, Minor League Player of the Year, and 2015 National League Rookie of the Year. Yet in 2016 he bettered all of those, winning the NL MVP Award. Tall, strong, versatile in the field, and preternaturally mature, he's on a path to have an epic baseball career.

"Q" is for Quirky–

That's Joe Maddon's style.
He gets his teams W's
And gets them to smile.

Joe Maddon is a baseball lifer with a light side and a deft managerial touch. As manager of the Tampa Bay Rays (2006–2014) he guided the small-payroll club to four playoff seasons and the 2008 American League pennant. In his two seasons in Chicago (2015 and 2016) he's led the Cubs to postseason berths and their best back-to-back records in more than 100 years. Maddon leavens his baseball savvy with wit, a sense of fun, and a penchant for lineup-juggling that keeps his teams alert through the long seasons.

"I want CRAZY in the Clubhouse every day. You need to be crazy to be great."
"TRY NOT TO SUCK."
"Don't ever Permit the PRESSURE to exceed the PLEASURE."
What's TRAVIS WOOD Doing in the Ivy?
Jon Lester Lays down a Pinch-Hit, Walk-off SQUEEZE BUNT!!!
Swapping Infielders with Outfielders in the MIDDLE OF AN Inning?

"R" is for Rizzo

Wise for his age.
He's helped the old franchise
Turn a new page.

Theo Epstein drafted an 18-year-old **Anthony Rizzo** when Theo was with the Red Sox in 2007, and, as a Cubs executive, acquired him from the San Diego Padres five years later. Over the next couple seasons, the sturdily built, left-handed-hitting first baseman developed from a prospect to a star. From 2014 to 2016, he's averaged more than 30 home runs and close to 100 runs batted in a season, while flashing Gold Glove–quality leather in the field. The young veteran has emerged as a leader of the young Cubs squad, both for his team spirit and tactical approach to hitting, and his off-field charity work has enhanced his status as a fan favorite.

"S" is for Santo

and Sandberg and Sosa
It's a letter the Cubs
Have sure made the most of.

Ron Santo, Ryne Sandberg, and Sammy Sosa are three of the all-time greatest Cubs. Santo was a nine-time All-Star third baseman in his 14 seasons with the team (1960–1973). Sandberg (1982–1997) was the best second baseman of his era and set a record for home runs by someone who played his position. Sosa, from the Dominican Republic, hit 60 or more home runs in each of three seasons—1998, 1999, and 2001—something no other player has done.

"T" is for Tape Measure,

There's often no trace
When young Kyle Schwarber
Blasts one into space.

Kyle Schwarber, sporting a Babe Ruthian girth and left-handed swing, has slugged since the moment the Cubs drafted him in 2014. His legend began to grow after a historic five–home run performance in the 2015 playoffs, before reaching epic levels in 2016, where an outfield collision resulting in torn knee ligaments seemingly ended his season in April. Schwarber, however, continued to amaze, returning to DH in the World Series, where he helped lead the Cubs to victory with a .500 OBP and 2 RBI.

"U" is for "Utility Man,"

A fellow who can play
More than one position
On any given day.

"V" is for "Hippo" Vaughn,

With the Cubs in the teens.
His left-handed deliveries
Stirred championship dreams.

Utility men are important parts of every major league team because of their versatility. By moving from position to position they allow managers to change their lineups in different ways. Jose Hernandez, normally a shortstop, played every position but pitcher or catcher for the 1998 Cubs.

James Vaughn, nicknamed "Hippo" because of his large frame, was the Cubs' best pitcher between 1913 and 1921, winning 20 or more games five times. In the 1918 World Series he gave up only three runs in three full games, but lost two of those because the Cubs were shut out. Babe Ruth, then a young Boston pitcher, won twice in that Series, which the Red Sox captured in six games.

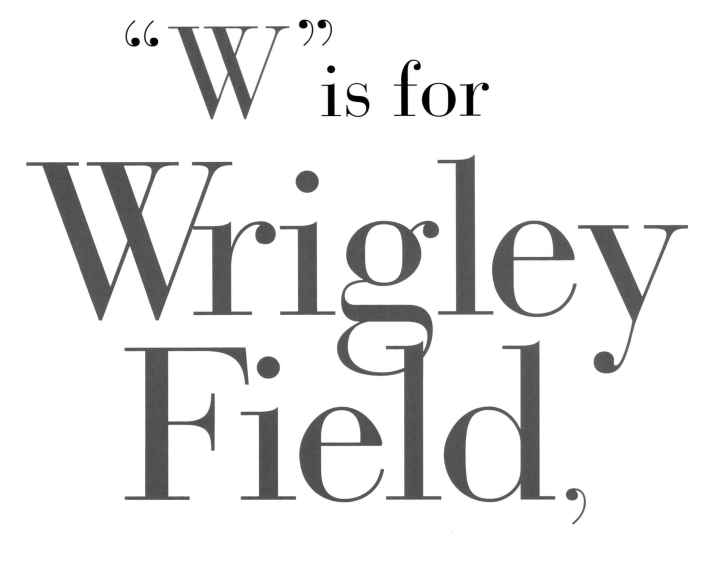

"W" is for Wrigley Field,

Which is where the Cubs play.
A prettier ballpark you won't find today.

Built in 1914, the Cubs' home is the Major Leagues' second-oldest stadium, behind only Fenway Park in Boston. It was first named Weeghman Park, then Cubs Park, and, since 1926, Wrigley Field, for the family that owned the team. Its ivy-covered walls and charming, metropolitan surroundings make it famous for its beauty.

There's an "X" in Jimmy Foxx
In fact, there are two.
He played with the Cubs
Before he was through.

The muscular Jimmy Foxx was one of baseball's all-time best power hitters, hitting 534 home runs over a 20-year period in the twenties, thirties, and forties. His best seasons were with the Philadelphia A's and the Boston Red Sox, but he also appeared with the Cubs in 1942 and 1944.

"Y" is for the

Year

Two thousand sixteen.
When the Cubs broke the drought
And realized the Dream.

"Z" is for Zeroes,

In the Cubs' foe's box score.
When Jake takes the mound
There's a "No-No" in store.

Jake Arrieta came to the Cubs in a little-noticed, 2013 trade with the Baltimore Orioles. In three-plus seasons in Baltimore the right-hander was regarded as a talented but erratic pitcher. But with the Cubs, Arrieta became the pitcher he was meant to be, winning the 2015 National League Cy Young Award while posting otherworldly numbers, including a 22–6 record with a 1.75 ERA. He also threw a no-hitter against the Los Angeles Dodgers on August 30. He continued to dazzle in 2016, adding another no-hitter against the Cincinnati Reds. He was the starting and winning pitcher in Games 2 and 6 of the 2016 World Series.

The illustrations in this book are dedicated to my son, Maxwell Willard Anderson.

Library of Congress Control Number: 2003117129

This book is available in quantity at special discounts for your group or organization.
For further information, contact:

Triumph Books
814 N. Franklin St.
Chicago, IL 60610
(312) 337-0747
Fax: (312) 337-5985

Printed in China
ISBN 978-1-62937-426-0